---- EXPLORING BIOLOGY ----

BIOLOGY OF THE HUMAN BODY

by
Tom Jackson

Minneapolis, Minnesota

Credits

Cover, © benschonewille/Adobe Stock; 3, © Anusorn Nakdee/Shutterstock; 4–5, © GraphicsRF.com/Shutterstock; 4T, © Yurchanka Siarhei/Shutterstock; 4B, © komkrit Preechachanwate/Shutterstock; 5B, © PeopleImages.com - Yuri A/Shutterstock; 6T, © VectorMine/Shutterstock; 6B, © murat photographer/Shutterstock; 6–7, © aslysun/Shutterstock; 7T, © Public Domain/Wikimedia Commons; 8B, © Katakari/Shutterstock; 8–9, © Grossinger/Shutterstock; 9T, © Designua/Shutterstock; 9B, © Public Domain/Wikimedia Commons; 10T, © gowithstock/Shutterstock; 10B, © Public Domain/Wikimedia Commons; 10–11, © Petro Shkvarok/Shutterstock; 11T, © Anatoliy Cherkas/Shutterstock; 12T, © Maryna Olyak/Shutterstock; 12B, © Manee_Meena/Shutterstock; 12–13, © Worldpix/Alamy Stock Photo; 13T, © StudioMolekuul/Shutterstock; 14T, © VectorMine/Shutterstock; 14B, © udaix/Shutterstock; 14–15, © Kateryna Kon/Shutterstock; 15B, © Public Domain/Wikimedia Commons; 16T, © Greentellect Studio/Shutterstock; 16B, © Designua/Shutterstock; 16–17, © Iokanan VFX Studios/Shutterstock; 17T, © Public Domain/Wikimedia Commons; 18T, © EugeneEdge/Shutterstock; 18M, © Kvitka Fabian/Shutterstock; 18B, © Lorraine Inglis/Shutterstock; 18–19, © CandyRetriever/Shutterstock; 19T, © Public Domain/Wikimedia Commons; 20B, © Valentina Antuganova/Shutterstock; 20–21, © Prostock-studio/Shutterstock; 21T, © EreborMountain/Shutterstock; 21B, © Public Domain/Wikimedia Commons; 22B, © Public Domain/Wikimedia Commons; 22–23, © YinYang/iStock; 23B, © hmardinal/Shutterstock; 24BL, © Designua/Shutterstock; 24BR, © Ken Welsh/Design Pictures/Science Photo Library; 24–25, © Mladen Mitrinovic/Shutterstock; 25T, © adriaticfoto/Shutterstock; 25B, © Public Domain/Wikimedia Commons; 26T, © Oleksandr Drypsiak/Shutterstock; 26M, © Biology Education/Shutterstock; 26B, © Neveshkin Nikolay/Shutterstock; 26–27, © aslysun/Shutterstock; 27TR, © Phonlamai Photo/Shutterstock; 27TL, © VectorMine/Shutterstock; 28T, © Peter Hermes Furian/Shutterstock; 28B, © Olga Popova/Shutterstock; 28–29, © Tridsanu Thopet/Shutterstock; 29ML, © Alex Mit/Shutterstock; 29MR, © DestinaDesign/Shutterstock; 30ML, © VectorMine/Shutterstock; 30MR, © Jose Luis Calvo/Shutterstock; 30B, © Public Domain/Wikimedia Commons; 30–31, © Air Images/Shutterstock; 31T, © Designua/Shutterstock; 32T, © Kermoal/BSIP/Science Photo Library; 32M, © Corbis/VCG; 32B, © VectorMine/Shutterstock; 32–33, © sutadimages/Shutterstock; 33B, © Public Domain/Wikimedia Commons; 34T, © solar22/Shutterstock; 34B, © Designua/Shutterstock; 34–35, © Maksim Denisenko/Shutterstock; 35T, © VectorMine/Shutterstock; 35B, © Michel Bakni/Wikimedia Commons; 36T, © cunaplus/Shutterstock; 36B, © peterschreiber.media/Shutterstock; 36–37, © Dragana Gordic/Shutterstock; 37B, © Stefan Albrecht/BioNTech/Wikimedia Commons; 38T, © VectorMine/Shutterstock; 38B, © VectorMine/Shutterstock; 38–39, © bbernard/Shutterstock; 39T, © German Vizulis/Shutterstock; 40B, © logika600/Shutterstock; 40–41, © Sebastian Kaulitzki/Alamy Stock Photo; 41T, © Suzanne Tucker/Shutterstock; 41B, © Public Domain/Wikimedia Commons; 42–43, © Monkey Business Images/Shutterstock; 42T, © Science History Images/Alamy Stock Photo; 42B, © New Africa/Shutterstock; 43B, © My Ocean Production/Shutterstock; 44B, © YinYang/iStock; 45T, © Mladen Mitrinovic/Shutterstock; 45B, © Kateryna Kon/Shutterstock; 47, © GraphicsRF.com/Shutterstock

Bearport Publishing Company Product Development Team

Publisher: Jen Jenson; Director of Product Development: Spencer Brinker; Editorial Director: Allison Juda; Editor: Cole Nelson; Editor: Tiana Tran; Production Editor: Naomi Reich; Art Director: Kim Jones; Designer: Kayla Eggert; Designer: Steve Scheluchin; Production Specialist: Owen Hamlin

Statement on Usage of Generative Artificial Intelligence

Bearport Publishing remains committed to publishing high-quality nonfiction books. Therefore, we restrict the use of generative AI to ensure accuracy of all text and visual components pertaining to a book's subject. See BearportPublishing.com for details.

Library of Congress Cataloging-in-Publication Data is available at www.loc.gov or upon request from the publisher.

ISBN: 979-8-89577-492-2 (hardcover)
ISBN: 979-8-89577-534-9 (paperback)
ISBN: 979-8-89577-500-4 (ebook)

© 2026 Arcturus Holdings Limited.
This edition is published by arrangement with Arcturus Publishing Limited.

North American adaptations © 2026 Bearport Publishing Company. All rights reserved. No part of this publication may be reproduced in whole or in part, stored in any retrieval system, or transmitted in any form or by any means, electronic, mechanical, photocopying, recording, or otherwise, without written permission from the publisher. Bearport Publishing is a division of FlutterBee Education Group.

For more information, write to Bearport Publishing, 3500 American Blvd W, Suite 150, Bloomington, MN 55431.

Contents

Understanding the Human Body 4
Studying Cells 6
Cell Membranes 8
Building Blocks 10
Enzymes 12
Cell Locomotion................... 14
Cell Division..................... 16
Homeostasis 18
Digestion and Excretion 20
Food and Diet 22
Respiratory System................. 24
Circulatory System 26
Skeletal System................... 28
Muscular System................... 30
Nervous System 32
The Senses 34
Immune System and Diseases 36
Reproductive System 38
Growth and Development............ 40
The Future of Researching the Body 42

Review and Reflect 44
Glossary.......................... 46
Read More........................ 47
Learn More Online................. 47
Index 48

Understanding the Human Body

Breathing and salivating may seem effortless. But these are extremely complex processes managed by millions of biological interactions happening every second! That's because the human body is constantly at work, helping people function throughout their everyday lives. Learning about the human body is a part of biology—the study of living things and their important processes.

Cells

Cells are the basic building blocks of all living things. At birth, a human has around 26 billion cells. This number increases as the baby grows older. One study found that the average 10-year-old is made up of around 17 trillion cells, and by the time they become an adult, their body contains more than 30 trillion cells.

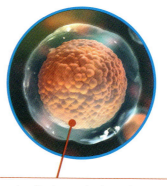

Every day, the human body produces billions of cells. When cells become damaged or die, the body makes new ones.

Organs

Organs work together to create the different biological systems that allow people to live and experience the world. The skin is the largest organ in the body. It makes up around 15 percent of a person's body weight.

The skin has three layers: the epidermis, dermis, and hypodermis. These layers are made of fats, minerals, protein, and water.

4

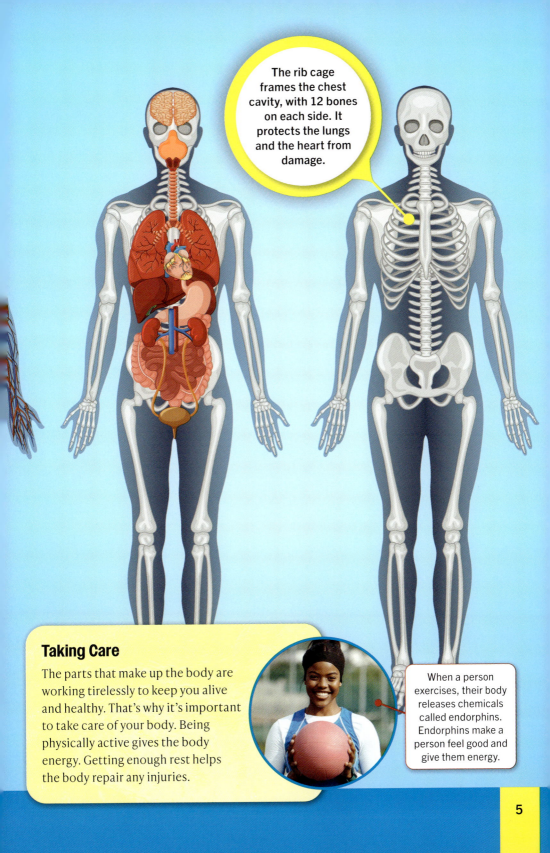

Studying Cells

One of the basic laws of biology is called cell theory. It says that every living thing has a body made of at least one cell—with many living things containing billions of cells—and every cell developed from an older cell. Looking more closely at cells helps scientists understand how the body works.

> Scientists who study cells are called microbiologists. They use electron microscopes to see samples in even more detail.

Light Microscopes

The main tool for studying cells is the light, or optical, microscope. It uses two sets of lenses to magnify tiny objects, allowing scientists to view them in detail. As light shines up through the sample, the first lens focuses the object into a tiny but detailed image. Then, the eyepiece and objective lenses magnify that image. This makes the picture big enough for the human eye to see.

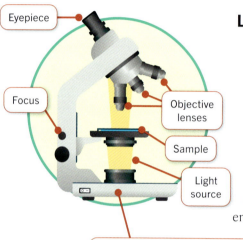

- Eyepiece
- Focus
- Objective lenses
- Sample
- Light source

A biological microscope usually has three objective lenses. Each one gives a different magnification level.

Preparing a Sample

The best way to examine cells is to place a thin slice of tissue on a clear glass slide. This slice is bathed in a droplet of water, and a see-through cover is placed on top. The cover holds the sample still and flat, which helps the lenses focus. Dyes are added to the water to highlight features of the sample. Salts and other chemicals can also be used to observe how the cells operate.

A thin sample allows for light to shine right through, which gives a clear picture of the silhouette of the cells.

HALL OF FAME

Margaret Pittman
1901–1995

As a child, Margaret Pittman assisted her father, who was a doctor, with his patients. Later, she attended the University of Chicago, where she became an expert in bacteria and microbiology. Pittman investigated the bacteria involved in deadly diseases, such as cholera and meningitis.

Scientists can adjust the brightness and position of the light source on a microscope to get a different view of samples.

A pipette is used to add dyes or other chemicals to samples.

DID YOU KNOW? A light microscope can see objects that are 200 times smaller than the width of a human hair.

Cell Membranes

Every cell is surrounded by a thin outer layer, or membrane. The membrane is made from fatty chemicals that form a barrier against large molecules. Smaller molecules, such as water and oxygen, can easily pass through. Cells rely largely on a physical process called diffusion, in which substances naturally spread out from areas of high to low concentration. However, some cells also use more active systems to move materials around.

Cell Movement

A cell that secretes hormones or enzymes uses exocytosis (*ek*-soh-sye-TOH-sis), which is when a cell releases large quantities of a substance. The substance is discharged by the cell's Golgi apparatus. This part of the cell transports, modifies, and packages proteins and lipids into small membrane bags called vesicles. The vesicle merges with the cell membrane, and the contents are outside the cell when they are released. Endocytosis (*en*-doh-sye-TOH-sis) is the reverse of exocytosis. The material outside a cell is captured in a hollow section of the cell membrane, which then breaks off to form a vesicle inside the cell.

Osmosis pulls water into plants. If there is not enough water in a plant's cells, the cells become soft, and the plant's body wilts.

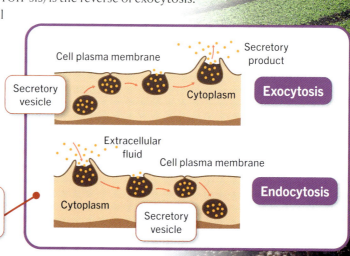

Endocytosis is used by cells that consume nutrients outside of the cells.

8   **DID YOU KNOW?** Goblet cells secrete slimy mucus to coat the inside of the nose, lungs, and throat. In an adult human, these cells produce almost 0.5 gallons (2 L) every day!

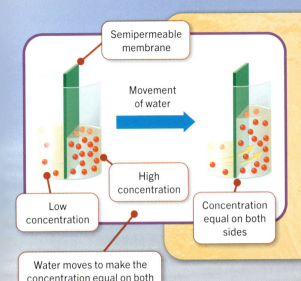

- Semipermeable membrane
- Movement of water
- Low concentration
- High concentration
- Concentration equal on both sides
- Water moves to make the concentration equal on both sides of the membrane.

Osmosis

Cells rely on osmosis, which is a special kind of diffusion, to move water into and out of cells. Water can cross the membrane, but other chemicals mixed with it cannot. When there is a high concentration of chemicals dissolved in the cell, water will diffuse in from outside to dilute it. If the cell is in water that is more concentrated than the cytoplasm, osmosis will push water out of the cell and dry it out.

Water is inside every cell, making it a universal solvent. All the chemicals needed for life are mixed into it.

Jean-Antoine Nollet
1700—1770

It would be impossible to understand how cells and living things work without Jean-Antoine Nollet. In 1748, he discovered osmosis by putting pure alcohol in a sealed pig's bladder that was immersed in water. Hours later, the bladder was bulging with water. Osmosis had pushed water inside to dilute the alcohol.

HALL OF FAME

Building Blocks

Cells and all living bodies are constructed from three main types of chemicals: carbohydrates, proteins, and fats. Carbohydrates are an easy source of energy, fats are used for long-term energy storage, and proteins are hardworking molecules that carry out life processes.

The rigid, strong parts of a plant, such as the trunk of a tree, are made of cellulose. This is a complex carbohydrate that is used in the cell walls of all plants.

Fats and Oils

Fats and oils, also called lipids, are produced by all life-forms. Animal fats are often waxy solids that hold more energy than plant fats, which are usually runny oils. A lipid molecule is built from three long acid molecules connected together. In solid fats, these molecules are highly tangled. While in an oil, the molecules can slip past one another.

Fried foods are cooked in hot oils. A fillet of fish is a major source of protein. Fried potatoes are a source of carbohydrates.

Many of the chemicals used by life, such as the ones in wood, are polymers. These chemicals are constructed from chains of smaller molecules linked together.

HALL OF FAME

Marie Maynard Daly
1921–2003

Marie Maynard Daly was the first Black American woman to be awarded a PhD in chemistry. Daly went on to study the biochemistry of cells and made discoveries about histones and cholesterol. Histones are proteins used to store deoxyribonucleic acid (DNA) in the nucleus, and cholesterol is a type of fat chemical used in the body. Daly showed that too much cholesterol was bad for a person's health.

DID YOU KNOW? Although the human brain makes up only 2 percent of the body's weight, it uses 20 percent of the body's total glucose supply each day.

Carbohydrates

The term *carbohydrate* is a combination of the words *carbon* and *hydrate*. As the name suggests, these chemicals are made from water and carbon. Carbohydrate molecules often have equal numbers of carbon and oxygen atoms and twice as many hydrogen atoms. This formula works for molecules of all sizes. Simple carbohydrates with small molecules, such as glucose and fructose, are called sugars. They taste sweet and are used as fuel for respiration. Starch is a complex carbohydrate made by chaining smaller glucose molecules together.

Honey is a thick, syrupy mixture of fructose, glucose, and water. Bees make it from nectar.

A tree's trunk has light and dark rings. Lighter rings are wider and show where plant cells have been growing fast during the summer. Dark rings show slow winter growth.

Cellulose and starch are polymers made from glucose. However, their glucose molecules are arranged differently. Cellulose forms tough strands used to construct a plant's body, while starch is soft and used as an energy store.

Enzymes

Metabolism refers to the chemical reactions that take place in a living cell. Most of these reactions are regulated by enzymes, which are chemicals that spur on reactions that would normally not happen by themselves. There are thousands of enzymes working in human cells.

Complex Shape

Enzymes are complex polymers that each have a uniquely intricate shape. Every enzyme has a specific job to do in metabolism, and that job is defined by the shape of the molecule. Its shape allows the enzyme to connect with other chemicals so they can react in some way. This idea is called the lock and key theory.

Fermented foods, like pickled vegetables, are made from enzymes released by yeasts or bacteria. The enzymes turn the sugars into acids, such as lactic acid or vinegars.

Protein molecules are made from two or three smaller polymers twisted around one another. The polymers are chains of smaller units called amino acids.

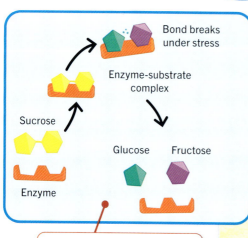

This enzyme is splitting a sucrose molecule into simple sugars.

Lock and Key

In the lock and key theory, an enzyme has a region called the active site that is shaped exactly right for other molecules, called substrates, to fit into—like a key in a lock. Once connected to the enzymes, the bonds inside the substrate molecules change in strength, allowing the atoms to rearrange themselves and create a new set of molecules. The resulting products are then released from the enzyme, leaving the enzyme ready to start the process again.

HALL OF FAME

AlphaFold
2021

An enzyme's shape is determined by the makeup of its amino acids. These small units are chained together in a specific order and push and pull on one another to fold up into the final protein shape. For a long time, nobody could figure out how to predict the shape of a protein from the order of its amino acids. Then, in 2021, an artificial intelligence program called AlphaFold figured this out. Now, it is easier to read genes, and artificial enzymes can be designed for use as medicines.

Fermented foods taste sour and acidic due to the action of enzymes.

The large amount of acid in fermented foods keeps other microscopic organisms from growing. This prevents food from rotting very quickly.

DID YOU KNOW? There are more than one million chemical reactions happening inside each of your cells every single second, and nearly every one requires an enzyme.

13

Cell Locomotion

The cells of many animals, protists, and some plants and fungi are on the move. The way they get around is called cell locomotion. This form of movement is used by cells to travel through water or over surfaces. Some cells are built for moving around the body. Others use their locomotion to create a current that pulls other materials toward them.

Flagella and Cilia

A common method of cell locomotion is to use extensions called flagella or cilia. Their motion creates a thrust force that pushes the cell along. The extensions move because of bundles of proteins inside a cell that slide back and forth, making the flagella and cilia bend and twist. Flagella are long whiplike extensions, while cilia are shorter and generally work together in large groups.

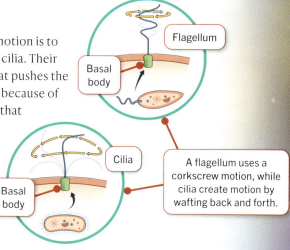

Flagellum

Basal body

Cilia

Basal body

A flagellum uses a corkscrew motion, while cilia create motion by wafting back and forth.

Amoeboid Motion

Cells without flagella or cilia move by extending the cell membrane into footlike appendages called pseudopodia. The pseudopodia shift forward, and the rest of the cell's contents flows into them. Because this is the way amoebas move, the motion is called amoeboid. However, it is not only amoebas that move like this. White blood cells defending the body from infection also use amoeboid movement to attack germs.

Pseudopodia spread out in all directions. Then, the cell will choose which one to flow into and move in that direction.

DID YOU KNOW? The lungs and windpipe are lined with ciliated cells that waft along a blanket of mucus to clear away dust and dirt that get into the airways.

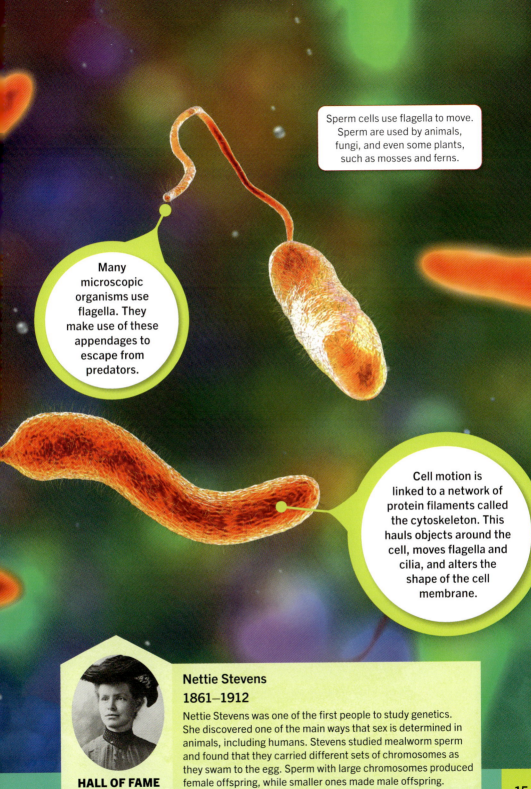

Cell Division

Cells can grow larger, but they all have a maximum size. In order for a body to grow beyond this point, its cells need to divide in two—again and again. The cell division process used for growth like this is called mitosis. It transforms one parent cell into two almost identical daughter cells. Complex cells, such as those of plants and animals, undergo mitosis. Bacteria use a similar system called binary fission.

> Between cell divisions, a cell is in interphase. During this time, the cell grows larger and organizes its chromosomes, getting ready for the next division.

Fast Growers

Cell division allows single-celled organisms to reproduce very quickly. For example, microscopic algae that float in seawater can double in number every 24 hours. Soon, there are so many that the plantlike organisms coat the water green! This explosion of life is called an algal bloom. It can spread poisons in the water and block light from reaching underwater plants.

Algal blooms are often caused by fertilizers washing into water. The chemicals make the algae grow and divide much faster than normal.

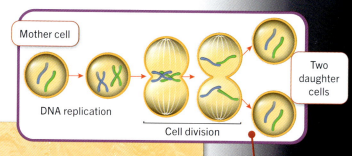

Mother cell
DNA replication
Cell division
Two daughter cells

Mitosis

Cell division by mitosis has several phases that ensure the daughter cells always have the same genes as the parent cell. The chromosomes in the nucleus are copied into double versions with an X shape. These are lined up in the middle of the cell, and then the two halves are pulled to opposite ends. Finally, a new cell membrane forms across the middle, splitting the cell into two.

> Each set of chromosomes is pulled to one end of the cell by microfilaments anchored there, separating the two sets. The chromosomes are divided equally between the two halves.

HALL OF FAME

Matthias Jakob Schleiden
1804–1881

Matthias Jacob Schleiden was one of the scientists behind cell theory. He had started work as a lawyer, but this made him unhappy—so he switched to studying cell biology. Schleiden showed that the contents of the nucleus were always shared by the new cells. He was one of the first biologists to accept Charles Darwin's theory of evolution.

In the final stage of cell division, known as cytokinesis, a new membrane forms in the middle of the cell, dividing up the cytoplasm.

Once cell division is complete, a new nucleus forms around the chromosomes in each cell.

DID YOU KNOW? A bacterium can split in half every 20 minutes. In just seven hours, one bacterium can grow into more than two million.

Homeostasis

All living bodies use a system called homeostasis to maintain stability. The human body is constantly working to keep internal conditions just right for its processes to function as well as possible. The system is mainly focused on keeping its temperature, water content, and chemical balance more or less constant.

Keeping Warm

A normal human body temperature is around 98 degrees Fahrenheit (37°C), which is usually warmer than the surrounding air. That means the body is always losing heat and must find ways of slowing that process to stay warm. When a person's body temperature falls too low, their muscles will start to twitch. This process is called shivering. These moving muscles give out warmth and help keep the body temperature from falling dangerously low.

Wearing thick clothes on a cold day helps trap a layer of air against the body. Heat moves slowly through this layer, so the body stays warm.

Goose Bumps

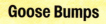

The human body is covered in hairs. These hairs usually lie flat and are hard for the human eye to see. However, when it's cold, each hair stands upright and makes small lumps on the skin called goose bumps. The upright hairs trap a layer of air against the skin, reducing heat loss.

A goose bump is created by a tiny muscle just below the surface of the skin. The muscle pulls on the hair shaft to make it straight, and that pushes up a bump on the surface.

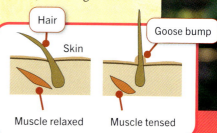

18

HALL OF FAME

Walter Bradford Cannon
1871–1945

Homeostasis was investigated by Walter Bradford Cannon around 100 years ago. He also described the fight-or-flight response, which is when the body switches from being relaxed to being ready to respond to danger. When this happens, a hormone called adrenaline is released. It changes the internal body conditions in a matter of seconds, redirecting energy to the muscles and senses.

Osmoregulation is the area of homeostasis involved in keeping the right amount of water in the body. The body becomes thirsty when it needs more water. Excess water is removed in urine.

On warm days, the body gets rid of extra heat by sweating. Water spreads over the skin and takes away the heat as it evaporates.

The blood vessels in the skin are involved in thermoregulation, or the control of body temperature. On cold days, they shrink in width. When less blood flows through the vessels, the skin turns pale. On warmer days, the vessels expand, letting more blood through. The skin becomes redder as this blood gives out its heat.

DID YOU KNOW? The human body can go without eating for three weeks before becoming very sick. However, the body cannot survive for longer than three days without water.

Digestion and Excretion

We need a frequent supply of chemicals for fuel to supply the body with the raw ingredients it needs for growing and maintaining body systems. These materials come from food, and the digestion process breaks down the food into useful substances. Waste materials are then removed through excretion.

Digestive Tract

Digestion turns the complex substances in food into simpler chemicals that can be absorbed by the body. This process takes place in the digestive tract, which is a long tube that passes through the body from the mouth to the anus. Enzymes break up the food, and its nutrients are absorbed into the blood in the small intestine.

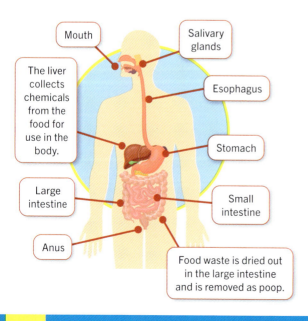

- Mouth
- Salivary glands
- The liver collects chemicals from the food for use in the body.
- Esophagus
- Stomach
- Large intestine
- Small intestine
- Anus
- Food waste is dried out in the large intestine and is removed as poop.

After swallowing, food is mashed up in the stomach. For about four hours, it is mixed with powerful chemicals that turn solid foods into a thick mushy liquid.

20   **DID YOU KNOW?** The small intestine is about 23 feet (7 m) long, while the large intestine is only about 5 ft. (2 m) long.

Excretion

Life processes taking place inside the body create waste products that have to be removed. The kidneys collect unwanted chemicals and turn them into urine. Urine travels along tubes to the bladder, where it is stored. When the bladder is about half full, the body gets the urge to pee, and the urine is emptied out.

Digestion starts as the teeth chew up food into smaller chunks. Saliva makes the balls of food smoother so they are easier to swallow.

HALL OF FAME

Santorio
1561–1636

It took 30 years of careful research for Italian scientist Santorio to find the link between food and digestion. He built a weighing chair to keep a record of his weight before and after every meal and every time he used the toilet. Santorio also weighed his meals, urine, and poop. His data showed that the weight of the food did not equal the weight of the waste. Some of the material from the food was going into his body.

21

Food and Diet

> These foods contain starch, which is a kind of complex carbohydrate. Simple carbohydrates are sweet sugars that combine into larger forms to make starchy foods, like bread and pasta.

Like all animals, humans survive by eating food. Food is made from the bodies of other living things, mostly plants, animals, and fungi. Whatever the source, food is made of the same kinds of chemicals that are useful to the body.

Food Groups

There are three main types of food: carbohydrates, fats, and proteins. Carbohydrates are used as the main source of energy for the body. Fats and oils are lipids, used by the body to store energy. Proteins are complex chemicals used inside every cell. The proteins in foods can be broken up and rebuilt into whatever protein the body needs.

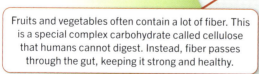

> Fruits and vegetables often contain a lot of fiber. This is a special complex carbohydrate called cellulose that humans cannot digest. Instead, fiber passes through the gut, keeping it strong and healthy.

HALL OF FAME

James Lind
1716–1794

James Lind was a Scottish naval doctor who demonstrated the importance of vitamins. After eating poor diets on long voyages, British sailors were dying from a disease called scurvy. Lind tried to determine which fresh fruits made people healthy and found that limes helped. It was later discovered that limes and other citrus fruits contain a lot of vitamin C, which prevents scurvy.

A human baby's first food is often milk. Some people drink milk from cows, sheep, and goats for their whole lives. They also eat other dairy products made from milk, such as cheese and yogurt.

Vitamins

The body is able to manufacture most of the chemicals it needs from the main food groups. However, it also needs a small but frequent supply of 13 vitamins. These are essential chemicals that are needed for the body to work properly but some of which cannot be made by the body. It is important to eat a wide range of fresh foods to get all the vitamins you need.

Meat is a good source of protein and fats. These food groups can be found in plants and mushrooms as well.

Many meals make use of grains, such as rice, corn, and wheat. They can be eaten as they are or made into breads, noodles, and pastas.

DID YOU KNOW? At least 1,900 species of insects are safe for humans to eat. Around two billion people worldwide regularly eat insects, including locusts and crickets.

23

Respiratory System

The body needs a constant supply of oxygen from the air. It is the job of the respiratory system to provide it. This system includes the airways and the lungs. Air coming into the lungs exchanges some of its oxygen with carbon dioxide, which is a waste gas that is breathed out.

Air entering the lungs is 21 percent oxygen. The air that comes out is only 16 percent oxygen.

Breathing Cycle

On average, you breathe in and breathe out every four seconds. The process is controlled automatically by a large muscle called the diaphragm (DYE-uh-*fram*). To inhale, the diaphragm flattens and stretches the lungs downward. Air flows in from the nose and mouth to fill the extra space. To exhale, the diaphragm bends upward and squeezes the air out.

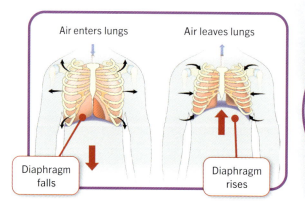

Air enters lungs — Diaphragm falls
Air leaves lungs — Diaphragm rises

Each lung is full of sacs called alveoli that are surrounded by blood vessels. Oxygen in the air moves to the alveoli and through the vessels into the blood. Carbon dioxide moves the opposite way, from blood to alveoli.

24 **DID YOU KNOW?** The world record for someone holding their breath underwater belongs to Budimir Šobat. In 2021, he held his breath for 24 minutes!

Coughs and Sneezes

When there is a blockage or an irritation of the airways, the body clears it with a cough or sneeze. It draws a big breath in and then closes off the airway using a flap in the throat called the epiglottis. With the epiglottis closed, the air pressure inside the lungs builds up. The force of the eventual release of air pushes the blockage out of the way.

A breath out includes water vapor from the moist lining of the lungs. This vapor forms little clouds on cold days.

During a sneeze, the tongue blocks the mouth and forces all the air out of the nose.

On average, a human breathes 2,970 gal. (11,240 L) of air every day.

Galen
129–216 CE

Galen treated wounded gladiators after deadly fights in the Colosseum in Rome. While doing his job, he often got to see inside of the human body. Galen was the first doctor to show how the lungs were connected to the throat by a windpipe, or trachea. He did this by using bellows to pump air into the lungs. Galen also identified the larynx, or voice box, at the top of the trachea.

HALL OF FAME

Circulatory System

The blood supply is the human body's transportation system, delivering oxygen and nutrients to all body parts and taking away the waste. The heart pumps blood around the body through blood vessels. Together, these body parts make up the circulatory system.

Exercising regularly helps the heart and circulatory system stay healthy. Any exercise that makes you feel tired strengthens this system.

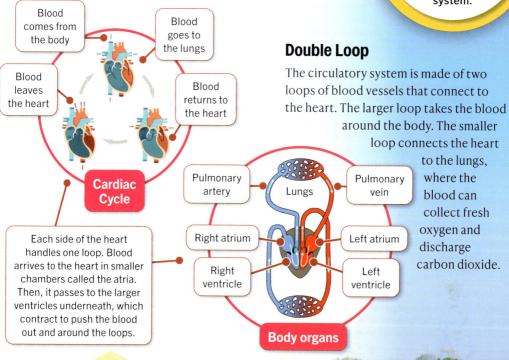

Double Loop

The circulatory system is made of two loops of blood vessels that connect to the heart. The larger loop takes the blood around the body. The smaller loop connects the heart to the lungs, where the blood can collect fresh oxygen and discharge carbon dioxide.

Each side of the heart handles one loop. Blood arrives to the heart in smaller chambers called the atria. Then, it passes to the larger ventricles underneath, which contract to push the blood out and around the loops.

HALL OF FAME

William Harvey
1578—1657

Ancient doctors believed that the blood spread out from the heart to be absorbed by the body and that new blood was being made all the time. William Harvey didn't think this made sense. At the time, he was not allowed to examine dead human bodies, so instead, he experimented with animals. In 1628, Harvey confirmed that blood circulates around the body in closed loops.

26

Blood Vessels

Blood is carried away from the heart by vessels called arteries. These vessels are lined with muscles that move in time with the heartbeat to push blood along. This can be felt as a pulse. Blood returns to the heart along veins, which have valves that open and close to ensure blood moves in only one direction.

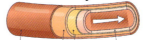

Artery

Outer layer | Smooth muscle | Elastic layer | Inner layer

Vein

Outer layer | Smooth muscle | Elastic layer | Inner layer

Most of the blood is made up of disk-shaped red blood cells. These carry oxygen using a red chemical called hemoglobin.

A normal resting heartbeat for an adult is between 60 and 100 beats a minute. Young people's hearts beat faster than those of adults.

A person's heartbeat and breathing rate both increase as they do more work. This ensures that the body takes in oxygen more rapidly to power the activity.

DID YOU KNOW? The average volume of human blood is about 11 pints (5 L). It takes 45 seconds for the heart to pump all of this blood around the body.

Skeletal System

At birth, we have 270 bones, but as we grow older, several smaller bones fuse together to make larger ones. By the time we are fully grown, there are only 206 bones. This skeletal system is the internal framework of the body. It is there to give the body its shape, to form a protective cage around the soft organs, and to create solid anchor points for muscles and ligaments.

The central core of the body makes up the axial skeleton. This holds 80 bones, including the flexible spinal column of 33 vertebrae, 24 ribs, and the skull. The skull is made of 22 bones fused together.

Joints

The place where two bones meet is called a joint. The human skeleton has 340 joints. Most of them are fixed and do not move. Joints that can move are called flexible or synovial joints. The bones here are connected by elastic straps called ligaments. There are six kinds of synovial joints in the human body—each able to move in different ways with twists, bends, and swivels.

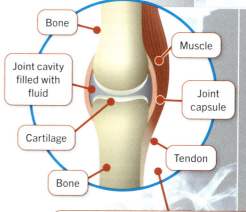

The places where the bones meet are surrounded by fluid-filled capsules. The tips of the bones are also padded with soft cartilage tissue.

HALL OF FAME

Mary Leakey
1913–1996

The Leakey family is famous for discovering fossils belonging to the distant ancestors of modern humans that lived in East Africa millions of years ago. Mary Leakey found the skeleton of an early relative of African apes that lived in the area about 20 million years ago.

28   **DID YOU KNOW?** The smallest bone in the body is called the stapes, or stirrup bone. It is 0.08 inch (2 mm) long and transmits sound through the ear.

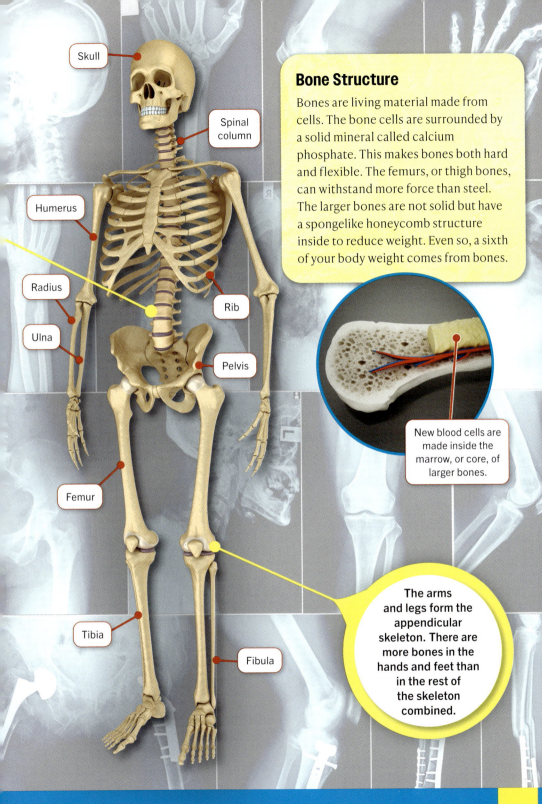

Bone Structure

Bones are living material made from cells. The bone cells are surrounded by a solid mineral called calcium phosphate. This makes bones both hard and flexible. The femurs, or thigh bones, can withstand more force than steel. The larger bones are not solid but have a spongelike honeycomb structure inside to reduce weight. Even so, a sixth of your body weight comes from bones.

New blood cells are made inside the marrow, or core, of larger bones.

The arms and legs form the appendicular skeleton. There are more bones in the hands and feet than in the rest of the skeleton combined.

29

Muscular System

There are hundreds of muscles in the human muscular system, consisting of three types. Cardiac muscle is found only in the heart, and it is constantly working. Smooth muscle is used in the gut, arteries, and other tubes of body systems. Lastly, the body has about 650 skeletal muscles that are used to move the body.

Muscles cannot contract forever. Their cells create lactic acid as they work. This acid makes muscles burn and feel tired. Eventually, all muscles must relax.

Moving Joints

Muscles create force by contracting, or growing shorter, to pull on the body. Skeletal muscles work in pairs to move joints, with one of the muscles contracting as the other stays relaxed. The flexor muscle contracts to bend the joint. On the other side of the joint, the extensor muscle contracts to straighten the joint.

Muscles are made up of billions of microscopic protein fibers bundled together.

Extensor contracts
- Biceps relaxed
- Joint straightens
- Triceps contracted

Flexor contracts
- Biceps contracted
- Triceps relaxed
- Joint bends

Muscles are attached to bones by tendons. These connectors are not very flexible, so they transfer all of the force from the muscles to moving the bones.

HALL OF FAME

Luigi Galvani
1737–1798

In 1780, Italian scientist Luigi Galvani found that frog muscles contracted as an electric current flowed through them. Galvani thought that electricity was made by the living force of an animal. The discovery led to the invention of the battery. Much later, it was shown how contractions were stimulated by the movements of electrical charges in muscle cells.

Smooth Muscle

The muscles that push food through the gut are smooth muscle. They are weaker than skeletal muscles. Smooth muscles are either longitudinal, meaning their fibers all line up, or are circular, with fibers in rings. These two types work together to create rhythmic waves of contractions in the gut that push food along.

Food • Esophagus • Sphincter • Stomach

The waves of contractions in the gut are called peristalsis. For this to work best, the food in the gut needs to contain solid fiber, so the muscles have something to push against.

Exercising muscles makes them bigger and stronger. When a muscle gets used, its fibers become a little damaged. The muscle repairs itself, adding more cells as it grows back bigger than before.

When a joint bends too much, the ligaments that connect the bones together become stretched. This injury is called a sprain. The best way to repair a ligament is to rest the joint.

DID YOU KNOW? The smallest muscle in the body is the stapedius muscle. This muscle in the ear is only 0.04 in. (1 mm) long and helps soften sounds.

Nervous System

The nervous system helps the various systems throughout the body communicate. It is made up of two parts. One is the central nervous system, which includes the brain and the spinal cord. The peripheral nervous system is a network of wirelike nerve cells that spread through the body. These nerve cells collect information from the senses and send it to the central nervous system. The brain sends responses to these messages back out through the nerves.

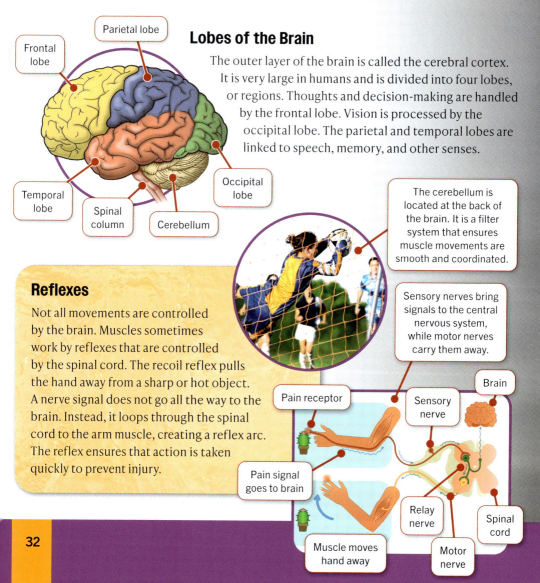

Lobes of the Brain

The outer layer of the brain is called the cerebral cortex. It is very large in humans and is divided into four lobes, or regions. Thoughts and decision-making are handled by the frontal lobe. Vision is processed by the occipital lobe. The parietal and temporal lobes are linked to speech, memory, and other senses.

The cerebellum is located at the back of the brain. It is a filter system that ensures muscle movements are smooth and coordinated.

Sensory nerves bring signals to the central nervous system, while motor nerves carry them away.

Reflexes

Not all movements are controlled by the brain. Muscles sometimes work by reflexes that are controlled by the spinal cord. The recoil reflex pulls the hand away from a sharp or hot object. A nerve signal does not go all the way to the brain. Instead, it loops through the spinal cord to the arm muscle, creating a reflex arc. The reflex ensures that action is taken quickly to prevent injury.

The outer region of the brain is mostly gray matter. This is where brain cells are closely packed together with many links between them.

The middle region of the brain is mostly white matter. The white comes from a fatty coating around the nerves that allows them to send signals faster. White matter forms the connections between areas of gray matter in the brain.

The base of the brain is called the brain stem. This is where the most basic body functions, such as breathing, swallowing, and regulating body temperature, are managed.

HALL OF FAME

Santiago Ramón y Cajal
1852–1934

It has been long known that the brain and nerves use electrical pulses to communicate, but Spanish microbiologist Santiago Ramón y Cajal discovered that there was no actual connection between any two nerve cells. Instead, there is a tiny gap called a synapse. Electrical pulses cannot pass across this gap. The nerves convert their signals into chemical messengers called neurotransmitters, which travel across the synapse.

DID YOU KNOW? If the human brain was a computer, it would have a storage capacity of 2.5 million gigabytes.

The Senses

The human body is said to have five senses: touch, sight, hearing, taste, and smell. These senses are constantly collecting information about what is going on inside and around the body. All this information is processed by the brain to create our awareness.

There are millions of touch receptors in the skin that pick up different kinds of forces pushing against them, such as sharp pricks or hard pressure.

Vision

The eye works to capture images. Light beams pass through the pupil and travel through a flexible lens that focuses the light to the retina at the back of the eye. Cells in the retina then stimulate nerve signals that together create a record of the image. This is sent along the optic nerve to the brain for processing.

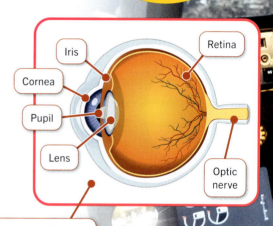

The iris can open and close to control the amount of light entering the eye. It opens wide in dark conditions and tightens up in bright light.

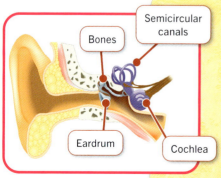

Hearing

Sound is the result of vibrating waves in the air. The ear is a highly sensitive touch organ that can pick up these waves and convert them into nerve signals. Sound waves enter the outer ear and make the eardrum vibrate. That vibration is passed to three tiny bones, which transfer it onto a spiral of fluid called the cochlea. The sound waves ripple through the cochlea, wafting hairlike nerve cells that send out signals to the brain.

DID YOU KNOW? The human nose rarely detects only one chemical at a time. It can recognize around 1 trillion distinct odors!

- Nasal cavity
- Smell receptors
- Nostril
- Mouth
- Tongue
- Windpipe

The senses of smell and taste use chemical detectors on the tongue and gums and inside the nasal cavity. The tongue can pick up at least five tastes, and the nose can pick up 10,000 distinct chemicals in the air.

The ear is also involved in the sense of balance. The brain detects changes in head position by how fluid shifts the semicircular canals in the inner ear. When this fluid gets churned up, we feel dizzy.

HALL OF FAME

Ibn al-Haytham
965–1040

Ibn al-Haytham, also known as Alhazen, was a medieval scientist from what is now Iraq. He showed that the eyes detect beams of light arriving from the surroundings. Before his work, most people believed that the eyes sent out invisible flashes that scanned objects and reflected back. However, he used mirrors and lenses to help show how light was focused inside the eye into a sharp image of the scene in front of it.

Immune System and Diseases

The body is under constant attack from other organisms that are trying to get inside it. Organisms that damage the body and cause diseases are called pathogens. This group includes bacteria, viruses, fungi, and even worms. The job of keeping pathogens out and hunting them down if they do get inside belongs to the immune system.

The immune system needs to work fast to fight pathogens. It raises the body's temperature, so the metabolism runs faster. A fever is a clear sign that someone is sick.

Clotting

The skin is the first line of defense against attack. Its outer layer is constantly shedding from the body and taking germs and dirt with it. Germs can get in through a cut in the skin. To defend against this, blood in the body will clot and form a solid patch over a cut called a scab.

A scab is a network of solid protein strands. It slowly dries out and flakes off as the skin underneath is repaired.

White Blood Cells

If pathogens get into the body, white blood cells find and destroy them. There are several kinds of white blood cells. Some produce chemical markers called antibodies that stick to the attackers. Other white blood cells then destroy anything with these markers. Memory cells keep a record of pathogens so they can be more easily dealt with if they infect the body again.

36 **DID YOU KNOW?** An allergy is caused by the immune system mistaking a harmless substance, such as pollen, for a pathogen and responding with an attack.

The immune system uses a lot of the body's energy, which is why being sick makes us feel tired.

Pathogens can spread to all parts of the body. The lymph system is a set of tubes running through the body that drains liquids from the muscles and organs and filters out pathogens.

HALL OF FAME

Ozlem Tureci
Born 1967

Ozlem Tureci is a German doctor who helped create vaccines for COVID-19, a disease that killed more than 7 million people between 2020 and 2024. Her vaccine taught a person's immune system how to fight back against COVID-19 so they would be less sick and less likely to die from the disease.

37

Reproductive System

A human baby develops inside its mother's uterus, or womb, before being born. This process starts when a male's sperm moves into a female's uterus and combines with an egg cell produced by the mother. Together, they make the first cell of a new human.

Doctors who look after mothers and children during pregnancy are called obstetricians. Midwives are also medical care-givers who are experts in helping people give birth.

Male Sex Organs

Sperm are produced inside the testes, which are egg-shaped organs inside the scrotum, a sac hanging beneath the penis. The sperm are transported along tubes to the prostate gland, where they are combined with liquid called semen. During intercourse, the penis is filled with blood. This makes it longer and harder so it fits into the vagina, where the semen and sperm are released.

- Seminal vesicle
- Prostate
- Bladder
- Vas deferens
- Urethra
- Testicle
- Penis
- Epididymis

The penis also contains a tube called the urethra that connects to the bladder. Urine leaves the body through the urethra.

- Fallopian tubes
- Ovary
- Fimbriae
- Cervix
- Uterus
- Vagina
- Endometrium

Fertilization

Most multicellular organisms reproduce sexually. This involves two types of sex cells, or gametes, fusing together in a process called fertilization. The female gamete is the egg, and the male one is the sperm. Together, they make the first cell of a new individual, called a zygote.

The opening of the uterus is called the cervix. During intercourse, the cervix allows sperm in. It becomes tightly closed once a fetus starts to develop in the uterus.

HALL OF FAME

Rebecca Lee Crumpler
1831–1895

In 1864, Rebecca Lee Crumpler became the first Black American woman to become a doctor. She was a specialist in child development and the care of women and babies after birth. She worked at a time after the U.S. Civil War (1861–1865) when people who had been formerly enslaved were being freed. Many white doctors would not treat people who had been enslaved, but Crumpler provided them with care.

Ultrasound scanners send high-pitched sounds into the uterus. The harmless sounds, which are too high to hear, echo off the fetus so the parents and medical experts can see it.

Human pregnancy lasts 40 weeks, or around 9 months. At this point, the baby can breathe air and live outside the mother but still needs a lot of looking after.

DID YOU KNOW? In 2021, Halime Cissé from Mali became the only mother of nonuplets in history when she gave birth to five girls and four boys.

39

Growth and Development

Girls reach their full adult size around the age of 15, while boys stop growing taller at around 18. And until about the age of 24, the brain and nervous system of both will continue to develop. The fastest period of growth is while a baby is still in the uterus. A single microscopic cell can develop into a 7-pound (3-kg) baby in 280 days.

> The fetus does not breathe or eat in the uterus. Instead, it is provided with what it needs by the placenta. Oxygen and nutrients move inside the placenta from the mother's blood to the baby's.

Three Trimesters

A baby developing inside the uterus is called a fetus. Its development happens in three-month stages, or trimesters. In the first trimester, the fetus develops all its body parts and organs. The fetus's body is mostly fully functional by the end of the second trimester. If it is born around this time, the baby could live—as long as it gets good medical care. The third trimester is devoted to growth and adding fat under the skin.

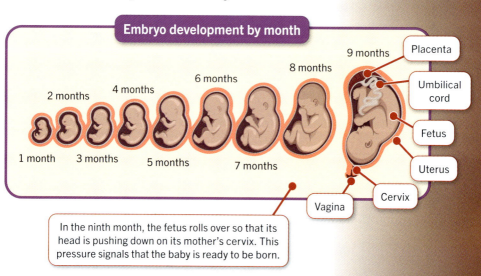

Embryo development by month

In the ninth month, the fetus rolls over so that its head is pushing down on its mother's cervix. This pressure signals that the baby is ready to be born.

40   **DID YOU KNOW?** Only 5 percent of babies are born on the exact day they are predicted to be due. The rest arrive early or late.

Childhood

In the first year after birth, a child will double in height and triple in weight! By the age of two, they are half their adult height. But a child may not reach half their adult weight until they are about 10.

The period of childhood occurs over the first 10 years for girls and 12 years for boys. Then, children enter puberty, where their growth speeds up again, and they develop adult body features.

For the second half of pregnancy, the fetus has a covering of fine hairs and slime. This falls off just before birth.

The umbilical cord connects the fetus to the placenta. This is cut after birth, and it falls away, leaving only a belly button.

HALL OF FAME

Cleopatra the Physician
1st century CE

Aside from being a doctor and writer, not a lot is known about Cleopatra of ancient Greece. She wrote one of the first books on gynecology, which is the medical study of the female reproductive organs. Cleopatra also wrote extensively on other ailments suffered by women and suggested using medicines, such as roasted horse teeth, mouse droppings, and deer bone, as cures.

The Future of Researching the Body

Biologists are constantly learning more about the human body. They hope to develop improved imaging technology that can more effectively view biological processes as they are happening. This will help biologists better understand how to prevent, treat, and hopefully cure harmful diseases so people can lead longer and healthier lives.

Researching Brain Disease

Alzheimer's disease destroys brain cells, which causes the brain to shrink. Currently, the illness kills about 1.8 million people worldwide each year. Scientists are working to develop new treatments, and researchers are looking for ways to slow down the disease's process or stop it entirely.

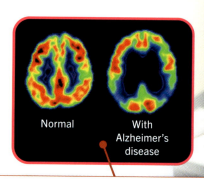

Normal | With Alzheimer's disease

This photo shows a brain scan of a normal brain and a brain with Alzheimer's. The brain with the disease is inflamed because of the buildup of toxic proteins.

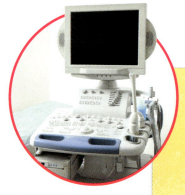

Ultrasound Technology

Ultrasound technology can currently view only larger body parts. However, scientists are using proteins that scatter sound to allow the technology to view the functions within tiny cells. With the help of artificial intelligence, they are working to assist in diagnostic support, enhance image quality, and provide accurate and efficient interpretations of results.

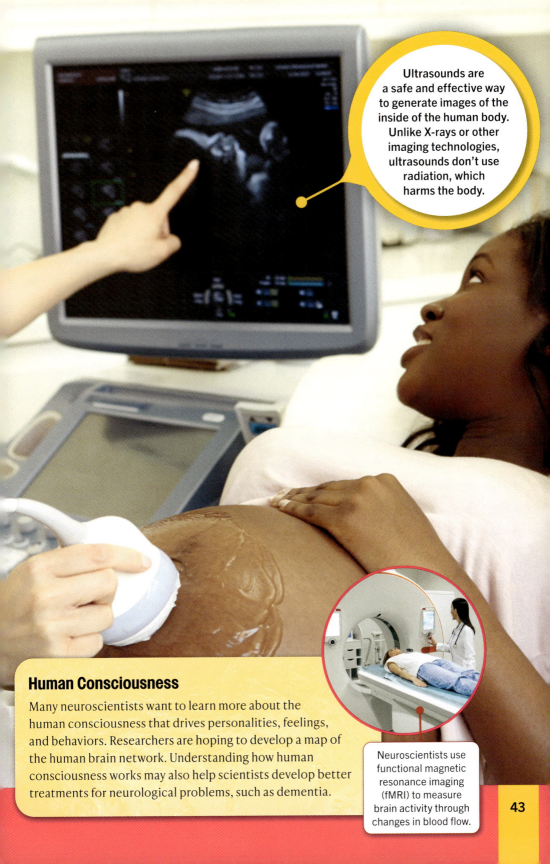

Ultrasounds are a safe and effective way to generate images of the inside of the human body. Unlike X-rays or other imaging technologies, ultrasounds don't use radiation, which harms the body.

Human Consciousness

Many neuroscientists want to learn more about the human consciousness that drives personalities, feelings, and behaviors. Researchers are hoping to develop a map of the human brain network. Understanding how human consciousness works may also help scientists develop better treatments for neurological problems, such as dementia.

Neuroscientists use functional magnetic resonance imaging (fMRI) to measure brain activity through changes in blood flow.

Review and Reflect

Now that you've read about the biology of the human body, let's review what you've learned. Use the following questions to reflect on your newfound knowledge and integrate it with what you already knew.

Check for Understanding

1. Name and describe the main tool used to study cells. *(See p. 6)*

2. What is a cell membrane and what does it do? *(See pp. 8-9)*

3. List and describe the three main types of chemicals that make up cells. *(See pp. 10-11)*

4. What regulates metabolism, and how does it work? *(See p. 12)*

5. Explain two ways that cells can move. *(See pp. 14-15)*

6. What is mitosis? How does it work? *(See pp. 16-17)*

7. How does the human body regulate temperature? What is this system called? *(See pp. 18-19)*

8. List three body parts used in digestion or excretion. Explain their role in the process. *(See pp. 20-21)*

9. Name and describe the three main types of food. *(See pp. 22-23)*

10. What system is made up of the lungs and airways? What does this system do? Name at least two other parts used in this system. *(See pp. 24-25)*

11. Which system moves blood throughout the body? List at least two parts used in this system and explain what they do. *(See pp. 26-27)*

12. Describe the relationship among bones, ligaments, joints, and cartilage. *(See pp. 28-29)*

13. List and describe the three types of muscles in the human body. *(See pp. 30-31)*

14. Name three parts of the brain and describe what each part does. *(See pp. 32-33)*

15. How does the human body protect itself from danger and disease? *(See pp. 36-37)*

Making Connections

1. Describe how bones, muscles, and blood work together in the body.

2. Which body parts or systems do each of the human senses use to gather information?

3. Choose two people mentioned in the Hall of Fame sidebars. What do they or their work have in common? What is one difference between them?

4. What role does skin play in the human body? Which systems does it work with?

5. Choose two systems described in the book. How do they work together? In what ways might they rely on each other?

In Your Own Words

1. In your opinion, which person described in the Hall of Fame sidebars did the most interesting or useful work? Why do you think so?

2. Which parts or system of the human body would you be most interested in learning more about? What questions do you have?

3. Which fact in this book surprised you the most? Why?

4. Scientists continue to study the human body. What areas do you think they should focus on? What do you wish we could learn?

5. Your body systems are working all the time. Which ones are you aware of as they are happening, and what do you notice or feel?

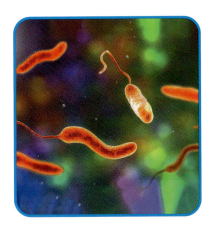

45

Glossary

amino acid an essential nutrient containing several chemical elements

bacteria a large group of single-cell microorganisms, some of which cause diseases

carbohydrates substances that contain carbon, hydrogen, and oxygen, such as a sugar or starch; these give the body energy

carbon dioxide (CO_2) a waste gas produced by the body, made up of one carbon atom bonded to two oxygen atoms

cell the basic building blocks of all living things

cellulose a substance that is the chief part of the cell walls of plants

digestion the process of breaking down food in the body to release essential nutrients

DNA the chemical ingredient that forms genes; parents pass on copied parts of their DNA to their children

enzymes chemicals that speed up or slow down the ways in which substances react with each other

fats chemical substances that the body produces to store energy

immune system the network of organs, chemicals, and special cells that protects the body from disease

membrane a thin, flexible layer of tissue around organs or cells

metabolism the chemical processes that the body's cells use to produce energy from food, get rid of waste, and heal themselves

nutrients substances that provide food needed for life and growth

organs groups of tissues that work together to do a specific job, such as the heart or brain

organisms living things, including plants, animals, fungi, and single-celled life-forms

protein one of the most important of all molecules in the body and in nature; protein is needed to strengthen and replace tissue in the body

respiratory system the set of organs that are responsible for helping the body with breathing

sperm a male reproductive cell that combines with a female's egg to produce a new baby

vein one of the main vessels carrying blood from different parts of the body to the heart

vitamins natural substances found in foods that the human body cannot produce

Read More

Cernak, Linda. *The Human Body Encyclopedia (Science Encyclopedias for Kids).* North Mankato, MN: Abdo Publishing, 2023.

Gagne, Tammy. *The Human Respiratory System (The Amazing Human Body).* San Diego, CA: BrightPoint Press, 2025.

McClure, Leigh. *The Human Body (The Inside Guide: Biology Basics).* Buffalo, NY: Cavendish Square Publishing, 2025.

Phillips-Bartlett, Rebecca. *Healthy Diet (Live Well!).* Minneapolis: Bearport Publishing Company, 2024.

Learn More Online

1. Go to **FactSurfer.com** or scan the QR code below.
2. Enter "**Biology Human Body**" into the search box.
3. Click on the cover of this book to see a list of websites.

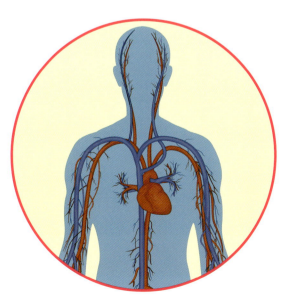

Index

babies 4, 23, 38–40
bacteria 7, 12, 16–17, 36
bones 5, 28–31, 34, 41
brain 10, 32–35, 40, 42–43
breathing 4, 24–25, 27, 33, 39–40
carbohydrates 10–11, 22
carbon dioxide 24, 26
cell division 16–17
cell membrane 8–9, 14–17
circulatory system 26
development 39–40
digestion 20–22
disease 7, 22, 36–37, 42
egg 15, 38
enzymes 8, 12–13, 20
exocytosis 8
eye 6, 18, 34–35
fats 4, 10, 22–23, 40
fertilization 38
food groups 22–23
growth 11, 13, 16–17, 20, 28, 30–31, 40–41
hearing 34, 39
homeostasis 18–19
immune system 36–37
joints 28, 30–31
ligaments 28, 31
locomotion 14
microbiologists 6, 33

microscopes 6–7
muscles 18–19, 24, 27–28, 30–32, 37
nervous system 32, 40
oxygen 8, 11, 24, 26–27, 40
penis 38
placenta 40–41
pregnancy 38–39, 41
proteins 4, 8, 10, 12–15, 22–23, 30, 36, 42
puberty 41
reflex 32
respiratory system 24
senses 19, 26, 32, 34–35
sex cells 38
skeleton 28–29
smell 34–35
sperm 15, 38
taste 11, 13, 34–35
tendons 28, 30
touch 34
urine 19, 21, 38
uterus 38–40
viruses 36
vitamins 22–23
water 4, 6, 8–9, 11, 14, 16, 18–19, 25
white blood cells 14, 36